Khurram Murad

The Islamic Foundation

Published by
The Islamic Foundation,
Markfield Dawah Centre,
Ratby Lane, Markfield,
Leicester LE67 9RN, UK

Quran House, PO Box 30611, Nairobi, Kenya

PMB 3193, Kano, Nigeria

© The Islamic Foundation 1997/1417 H.

First published 1997

ISBN 0 86037 273 1

British Library Cataloguing in Publication Data
A Catalogue card for this book is available from the British Library

Typeset in Baskerville 11/14

Printed and bound in Great Britain by the Cromwell Press

Preface

What does the Prophet Muhammad teach?

For centuries his teachings have been bringing light and peace to countless people, enlivening the hearts and lives of billions of men and women down the ages. Him they have loved more dearly than their own selves, in him they have found their greatest source of inspiration and guidance, he has been the ultimate norm and the perfect example for them, he has been their mainstay in personal vicissitudes and tribulations, his teachings have led them through social and political turmoils as well, he has inspired them to greater and greater heights of spiritual and moral upliftment and civilizational achievements – in short, through him God has spoken to them, He has been with them.

He lived all his life in the full glare of history. Those who loved him and followed him have preserved even the minutest details of how he lived, what he did, and what he said.

It is important to know what he did teach. However, many people in the world today hear very little of his teachings. These teachings are as little known, as much misunderstood, as he himself. Yet they contain immense treasures of wisdom which, once discovered, may bring new life to individuals, communities, indeed to humanity at large. These teachings bring precious and wonderful gifts of godliness and brotherhood, love and peace, mercy and justice, kindness and fairness, generosity and forgiveness, humility and self-dignity.

Out of a vast treasure house of such priceless gifts we have selected a few, and arranged them here under forty topics. We hope that they will serve as an inviting introduction to all, especially those who are not familiar with the Prophet or those who do not believe in him as a prophet. May his gifts bring warmth and light, peace and happiness to a world which has lost its sense of direction and purpose, has become devoid of compassion, justice and forgiveness, and is plagued by discord, hatred, injustice and violence.

Finally, I pray to Allah, *subhanahu wa ta'ala,* to accept this humble effort to make the teachings of His last Messenger reach a wider audience, and forgive my shortcomings and mistakes.

Leicester   **Khurram Murad**
18 Jamadius Sani 1417
1 November 1996

1
The Most Merciful God

1
God's Mercy

The Messenger of God, blessings and peace of Allah be upon him, said: 'When God decided upon to create, He also pledged Himself to be merciful to all His creation, by writing in His Book which is with Him above His Throne, "My mercy shall prevail over My anger." '

(*Bukhari, Muslim*: Abu Hurayrah)

The Messenger of God, bpuh, said: 'If believers knew the severity of God's punishment, no one would hope to enter His Paradise; and if disbelievers knew the vastness of His mercy, no one would despair of entering His Paradise.'

(*Bukhari, Muslim*: Abu Hurayrah)

Once we were with the Prophet, bpuh, when a man came forward, who held in his hand something wrapped up in a blanket. He said: 'O Messenger of God, I was passing by a thicket of trees when I heard some young birds chirping. I seized them and put them in my blanket. Then their mother appeared and began to hover over my head. So I uncovered them a little to let her see. She alighted on them, and I wrapped them all up in my blanket. Here they all are.'

The Prophet, bpuh, immediately ordered them to be put down. I put them down, but their mother would not leave them. The Prophet, bpuh, thereupon, said: 'Do you wonder at the compassion of this bird for her young? By Him who has sent me with the Truth, God is more merciful to His servants than this mother of young birds is to her young.'

Then he ordered: 'Take them back and put them where you got them. And their mother as well.' So he took them back.

(Abu Dawud: 'Amir al-Rami)

2
Let There Be No God But God

The Prophet, bpuh, said: 'The right of God upon His servants is that they worship and serve Him alone, and make none a god beside Him; and the right of servants upon God is that He does not punish those who do not make anything a god beside Him.'

(Bukhari, Muslim: Mu'adh)

Once we were with the Prophet, bpuh, on one of his expeditions, when we came upon certain people. He asked them who they were. They said that they were Muslims. Among them was a woman who had a child with her. She was kindling a fire, and when the flames rose, she moved her child away.

She went to the Prophet, bpuh, and asked, 'Are you God's Messenger?' He said, 'Yes, I am.' She, then, said, 'You for whom I would give my father and mother as ransom, tell me if God is not the most merciful of all who are merciful?' He said, 'Yes, He is.' She, then, asked, 'Is God not more merciful to His servants than a mother to her child?' He said, 'Yes, He is.' She, then, said, 'But a mother does not throw her child into fire.'

On hearing this, the Prophet, bpuh, bowed his head and wept. Then he raised it, looked at her, and said, 'God would not punish any of His servants except the one who is bent upon denying and rebelling against Him and refuses to say "there is no god but God." '

(*Ibn Majah*: Abdullah ibn Umar)

3
Utter Dependence Upon God

The Prophet, bpuh, said: God says, 'My Servants, I have forbidden Myself doing any wrong and have also forbidden you, so do no wrong unto one another.

'My servants, all of you are astray except those whom I guide; so ask Me for guidance and I shall guide you. My servants, all of you are hungry except those whom I feed; so ask Me for food and I shall feed you. My servants, all of you are naked except those whom I clothe; so ask Me for clothing and I shall clothe you. My servants, you sin by night and by day, yet I forgive all sins; so ask Me for forgiveness and I shall forgive you.

'My servants, you can do nothing that could harm Me, neither can you do anything that would benefit Me.

'My servants, even if the first and the last of you, all the human beings and the jinn, become as righteous as the one with the most righteous heart among you, that would add nothing to My kingdom. My servants, if . . . [all of you] . . . become as wicked as the one with the most wicked heart among you, that would diminish nothing from My kingdom.

'My servants, were . . . [all of you] . . . to stand in one place and ask Me whatever you wished, and were I to give everyone what he asked for, that would not diminish what I have any more than a needle would when put into a sea.

'My servants, it is only your deeds which I put into your account, and then pay you in full for them; so let him who finds good thank and praise God, and let him who finds other than good blame no one but himself.'

(*Muslim*: Abu Dharr)

4
The Prophet: God's Mercy and Guidance

The Prophet, bpuh, said: 'I have been told a parable about myself: A lord built a house, laid a feast in it, and sent an emissary to invite everybody to the feast. Anyone who accepted his invitation, he entered the house, ate of the feast, and earned the lord's pleasure; but the one who did not accept his invitation, he did not enter the house, got no share of the feast, and incurred the lord's anger.'

He, then, explained thus: 'The lord is God, the emissary who issues the invitation to the feast is Muhammad, the house is Islam, and the feast is the Paradise.'

(*Darimi*: Rabi'a al-Jurashi)

The Messenger of God, bpuh, said: 'I am like a man who kindled a fire, and when it lit up the place, the moths and the creeping insects began to fall into it. He tried to prevent them, but they got the better of him and rushed into it. You and I are like that. I am seizing your girdles to pull you away from the Hell-fire: "Come away from the Fire! Come away from the Fire." But you are getting the better of me and rushing into it.'

(*Bukhari, Muslim*: Abu Hurayrah)

5
God's Unbounded Forgiveness

The Messenger of God, bpuh, said: God says, 'Son of Adam, so long as you keep calling upon Me and hoping for good from Me, I shall forgive you whatever you have done, and I care little. Son of Adam, were your sins to rise as high as the sky, and were you then to ask Me for forgiveness, I would forgive you. Son of Adam, were you to come to Me with sins as large as would fill the earth, and meet Me having ascribed no partner to Me, I would bring you forgiveness as great as your sins.'

(*Tirmidhi*: Anas)

The Prophet, bpuh, said: 'All children of Adam are sinners, but best among sinners are those who constantly repent.'

(*Tirmidhi*: Anas)

The Messenger of God, bpuh, said: 'One is not counted as a persistent sinner if he seeks forgiveness

every time he sins, even if he returns to the same
sin seventy times a day.'

(Tirmidhi, Abu Dawud: Abu Bakr)

The Messenger of God, bpuh, said: 'By Him
who has my soul in His hands, were you not to sin,
God would have removed you, and brought another
people who would sin, then ask for God's
forgiveness, and God would forgive them.'

(Muslim: Abu Hurayrah)

The Messenger of God, bpuh, said: 'When a
believer sins, a black spot appears on his heart. But
if he repents and seeks Allah's forgiveness, his heart
becomes cleansed and polished. However if he
continues to commit more and more sins (without
seeking forgiveness), the spot continues to spread
and ultimately covers all of his heart. This is the
rust which God mentions [in the Qur'an]: "*What
deeds they earn rust upon their hearts.*" '

(Ahmad, Tirmidhi: Abu Hurayrah)

6
God's Generous Reckoning

The Messenger of God, bpuh, said: 'God records the good deeds and the bad deeds thus: If anyone intends to do a good deed but does not actually do it, God writes it down with Him as a full good deed. If he intends it, and does it too, God writes it down with Him as ten to seven hundred times that good deed, or many times over. If anyone intends to do a bad deed but does not actually do it, God writes it down with Him as a full good deed. When he intends a bad deed and does it as well, only then God writes it down as one bad deed.'

(*Bukhari, Muslim*: Ibn 'Abbas)

The Messenger of God, bpuh, said: 'God has, for my sake, pardoned my people for all acts they do mistakenly, forgetfully, or under duress.'

(*Ibn Majah*: Ibn 'Abbas)

2
Seeking Godliness

7
Heart: The Source of All

The Messenger of God, bpuh, said: 'Listen carefully, there is a lump of flesh in the body. If it is set right and made good, the entire body becomes good and healthy; but if it becomes diseased, the entire body becomes diseased. Remember well: it is the Heart.'

(*Bukhari, Muslim*: Nuʿman ibn Bashir)

The Messenger of God, bpuh, said: 'If someone wants to know what position he enjoys in the eyes of God, he has only to look at what place he gives to God [in his heart and life].'

(*Hakim*: Jabir)

The Messenger of God, bpuh, said: 'A Muslim is a Muslim's brother; he does not wrong him, nor desert him, nor looks down upon him. Remember, piety lies here! (And he pointed his finger to his heart three times.) To belittle one's Muslim brother [in thoughts or treatment] is enough of evil for a person to do.'

(*Muslim*: Abu Hurayrah)

8
Living in God's Presence

Once the Prophet, bpuh, was asked: 'Tell us what is excellence (iḥsān)?'

He said: 'Excellence is that you worship and serve God (in all your life) as though you are seeing Him; for He always sees you, even if you do not see Him.'

(*Bukhari, Muslim*: Umar ibn al-Khattab)

Someone asked: 'How can one purify and develop himself, O Messenger of God, bpuh?

He replied: 'He should always remember that God is with him wherever he is.'

(*Tirmidhi*: Abdullah ibn Busr)

The Prophet, bpuh, said: 'Remain conscious of God and fear Him wherever you are, and follow a bad deed with a good deed which will wipe it out, and behave well towards people.'

(*Tirmidhi*: Abu Dharr)

One day I was riding behind the Prophet, bpuh, when he said to me: 'Young man, shall I teach you some words [of advice]: Be mindful of God's (commands) and God will protect you. Remember God and you will find Him in front of you. [Know God in prosperity and He will know you in adversity.] If you have to ask, ask of God; if you have to seek help, seek help from God. Remember that if all the people were to join hands to bring you some benefit, they cannot bring you any benefit except that which God had already decreed for you. And if they all were to join hands to harm you, they would harm you only with that which God had already decreed for you. The pens have been lifted and the pages have been dried.'

(*Tirmidhi*: Ibn 'Abbas)

9
Remembering and Nearing God

The Prophet, bpuh, said: God says, 'I treat My servant as he hopes that I would treat him.

'I am with him whenever he remembers Me. If he remembers Me in his heart, I remember him in My "heart"; and if he remembers Me in a gathering, I remember him in a gathering far better than that gathering.

'And if he draws near to Me a hand's span, I draw near to him an arm's length; and if he draws near to Me an arm's length, I draw near to him a fathom's length. And if he comes to Me walking, I go to him running.'

(Bukhari, Muslim: Abu Hurayrah)

The Messenger of God, bpuh, said: 'One who remembers God and one who does not are like the living and the dead.'

(Bukhari, Muslim: Abu Hurayrah)

10
Seeking God's Love

The Messenger of God, bpuh, said: 'Anyone who possesses three qualities finds thereby the sweetness of faith: that he loves God and His Messenger, bpuh, more than everything else; that when he loves a human being he loves him for God's sake alone; and, that he abhors returning to unbelief from which God has rescued him, as he abhors being thrown into fire.'

(Bukhari, Muslim: Anas)

The Messenger of God, bpuh, said: 'God has said: "I love nothing more than that My servant should draw near to Me by performing duties I have enjoined upon him. Then when My servant desires to be near to Me so much that he does voluntary good deeds as well, I love him so much so that I become his 'ears' with which he hears, his 'eyes' with which he sees, his 'hands' with which he works, and his 'feet' with which he walks. Were he to ask of Me something, I would surely give it to him; and were he to seek refuge with Me, I would surely give him refuge." '

(*Bukhari*: Abu Hurayrah)

The Prophet, bpuh, said: 'Anyone who wants to be true in his love for God and His Messenger, or desires that God and His Messenger should love him, he should always speak the truth, fulfil all trusts entrusted to him, and be a good neighbour.'

(*Baihaqi*: Abdur Rahman ibn Abu Qurad)

A man came to the Prophet, bpuh, and asked: 'O Messenger of God, tell me of some deeds which I may do, so that Allah will love me as well as people will love me.'

He said: 'Do not covet this world, and Allah will love you; do not covet what people possess, and people will love you.'

(*Ibn Majah*: Sahl ibn Saʿd)

11
Finding God by Serving Mankind

The Messenger of God, bpuh, said: God will say, 'Son of Adam, I fell ill but you did not visit Me.' He will say, 'O Lord, and how could I have visited You! You are the Lord of the worlds!' He will say, 'Did you not know that My so-and-so servant had fallen ill and you did not visit him? Did you not know that had you visited him you would have found Me with him?'

'Son of Adam, I asked you for food but you did not feed Me'. He will say, 'O Lord, how could I have fed You! You are the Lord of the worlds!' He will say, 'My so-and-so servant asked you for food and you did not feed him? Did you not know that had you fed him you would surely have found that with Me?'

'Son of Adam, I asked you to give Me to drink but you did not give Me.' He will say, 'O Lord, how could I have given you to drink! You are the Lord of the worlds!' He will say, 'My so-and-so servant asked you to give him to drink and you did not give him. Had you given him to drink you would surely have found that with Me'.

(*Muslim*: Abu Hurayrah)

12
Outward Religiosity and Ostentation

The Messenger of God, bpuh, said: 'Many a one fast, but gain nothing from their fasting except hunger and thirst; and many a one pray all night, but gain nothing from their night prayers except sleeplessness.'

(*Darimi*: Abu Hurayrah)

The Messenger of God, bpuh, said: 'If one does not abstain from falsehood, and acting in accordance with it, God is in no need of his abstaining from food and drink.'

(*Bukhari*: Abu Hurayrah)

A man came to the Prophet, bpuh, and asked: 'One fights for booty, one for the sake of reputation, and one to show off his bravery: which of them is fighting in God's cause?'

The Prophet, bpuh, said: 'Only the one who fights so that God's guidance may prevail, fights in God's cause.'

(*Bukhari, Muslim*: Abu Musa)

The Messenger of God, bpuh, said: 'Whoever prays to show off, he is [a sort of] idolater, for he makes a god beside God; whoever fasts to show off, he also makes a god beside God; and whoever gives charity to show off, he too makes a god beside God.'

(*Ahmad*: Shaddad ibn Aws)

13
Hypocrisy

The Messenger of God, bpuh, said: 'Three characteristics are the signs of a hypocrite, even if he fasts, performs the Prayer and claims that he is a Muslim: when he speaks, he lies; when he makes a promise, he breaks it; and when he is trusted, he betrays his trust.'

(*Bukhari, Muslim*: Abu Hurayrah)

The Messenger of God, bpuh, said: 'A man will be brought to the Fire on the Day of Judgement, and he will be thrown into it. His guts will spill out in it, and he will go round and round like a donkey at a mill. The people in the Hell-fire will gather round him and say, "Oh, you! What is the matter with you? Did you not use to tell us to do good and forbid us to do evil?" He will say, "Yes, I used to tell you to do good, but did not do it myself; and I used to forbid you from evil, but I did it myself." '

(Bukhari, Muslim: Usama)

14
Golden Rules for Obedience

The Messenger of God, bpuh, said: 'God has laid down certain duties, so do not neglect them; He has set certain boundaries, so do not overstep them; He has prohibited certain things, so do not violate them; about the rest of things He has kept silent – out of compassion for you, not because He has forgotten [or made a mistake] – so leave them alone and refrain from questioning about them.'

(Daraqutni: Abu Tha'labah)

The Messenger of God, bpuh, said: 'What I have forbidden to you, avoid; what I have enjoined upon you, do as much as you can. It was only excessive questioning and then following paths different from what their Prophets told them that destroyed those who were before you.'

(*Bukhari, Muslim*: Abu Hurayrah)

The Messenger of God, bpuh, said: 'That Muslim is guilty of the most serious offence who enquires about something which is not forbidden for men, but is declared forbidden because of his questioning.'

(*Bukhari, Muslim*: Sa'd ibn Abi Waqqas)

I asked the Messenger of God, bpuh: 'What is virtue and what is sin?' He said, 'Virtue is to have good morals, sin is what pricks your heart and you dislike that people come to know about it.'

(*Muslim*: Nawas ibn Sam'an)

The Messenger of God, bpuh, asked me: 'Have you come to ask about virtue?' I said, 'Yes.' He said, 'Seek a verdict from your Heart. The virtue is that about which your soul and heart feel satisfied. Sin is that which troubles the soul and about which the heart is uneasy and confused, even though people may again and again give their legal opinions in its favour.'

(*Muslim*: Wabisa ibn Ma'bid)

The Prophet, bpuh, said to Abdullah ibn 'Amr: 'Have I heard right that you fast every day and stand in prayer all night?' Abdullah replied, 'Yes, O Messenger of God.' The Prophet, bpuh, said, 'Do not do that. Fast, as well as eat and drink. Stand in prayer, as well as sleep. For your body has a right upon you, your eyes have a right upon you, your wife has a right upon you, and your guest has a right upon you.'

(*Bukhari, Muslim*: Abdullah ibn 'Amr)

When the Prophet, bpuh, came to Madinah, people used to cross-fertilize the date-palm trees in a particular manner. He asked them, 'Why are you doing it?' They replied, 'This has for long been our practice.' He said, 'Maybe it would be better if you do not do it.' So they gave it up, but the crop was reduced. They mentioned this to him, whereupon he said, 'I am only a human being. If I tell you anything about Islam, obey it. But when I instruct you about anything based upon my opinion about worldly business, then I am only a human being and you know your worldly business better.'

(*Muslim*: Rafi' ibn Khadij)

3
Mercy and the Way
of Giving

15
Mercy to God's Family

The Messenger of God, bpuh, said: 'All creatures are God's family; and God loves them most who treat His family well and kindly.'

(*Baihaqi*: Anas)

The Messenger of God, bpuh, said: 'Only those who are merciful will be shown mercy by the Most Merciful. Show mercy to those who are on earth, He who is in heaven will show mercy to you.'

(*Abu Dawud, Tirmidhi*: Abdullah ibn 'Amr)

The Messenger of God, bpuh, said: 'God will not show mercy to him who does not show mercy.'

(*Bukhari, Muslim*: Jabir ibn Abdullah)

The Messenger of God, bpuh, said: 'Forgiveness was granted to a prostitute! She came upon a dog at the mouth of a well, who was panting and was about to die of thirst. She took off her leather sock, tied it with her headscarf, and drew some water from the well for the dog. It was for this act of kindness that she was forgiven her sins.'

When asked, 'Are we rewarded even for good we do to animals?' he replied, 'Reward is given for good done to any living creature.'

(*Bukhari, Muslim*: Abu Hurayrah)

16
The Garden of Charity

The Messenger of God, bpuh, said: 'Every Muslim must give charity.'

Some people asked: 'What if he has no money?'

He replied: 'He should work with his hands, and meet his needs as well as give charity to others.'

They asked: 'What if he could not, or did not, do that?'

He replied: 'Then he should assist a needy person in distress.'

They asked: 'What if he could not do that as well?'

He replied: 'He should then teach good things.'

They asked: 'And, if he could not do even that?'

He replied: 'Then, he should refrain from harming anyone. That, too, would be charity on his part.'

(*Bukhari, Muslim*: Abu Musa al-Ash'ari)

The Messenger of God, bpuh, said: 'Giving charity is incumbent upon every bone of every human being every day that the sun rises: To judge fairly between two people is charity. To help someone mount his animal is charity. To help someone load his pack is charity. To say a good word is charity. To remove any harmful thing from the road is charity.'

(*Bukhari, Muslim*: Abu Hurayrah)

17
This Too is Charity!

The Messenger of God, bpuh, said: 'Every time you say "glory be to God", it is charity; likewise every "God is great" is charity; every "all praise be to God" is charity; every "there is no god but God" is charity; every act enjoining good is charity; every act of forbidding evil is charity; and sexual intercourse with one's wife is also an act of charity.'

Surprised, they asked if a reward would be given even for satisfying one's desire. He said, 'Tell me, if he were to satisfy it in an unlawful manner, would it not be a sin? So, if he were to satisfy it lawfully, he would have a reward.'

(*Muslim*: Abu Dharr)

The Messenger of God, bpuh, said: 'When a Muslim spends to support his family, and hopes to be rewarded for it, it is a charity for him.'

(*Bukhari, Muslim*: Abu Hurayrah)

The Messenger of God, bpuh, said: 'If a Muslim plants a tree or sows a crop, then whatever bird eats of it, or a human being, or an animal, it counts as charity for him. He also said: 'Whatever is stolen from it, that too counts as charity.'

(*Bukhari, Muslim*: Anas, Jabir)

The Prophet, bpuh, said: 'A man was in a waterless plain when he heard a voice from a cloud, "Water so and so's garden." The cloud moved on and poured its water on a rocky land, which flowed into a channel. The man followed the water and came upon a man standing in his garden and diverting the water into it with his spade.

'The man asked the gardener, "What is your name?" He told him his name, which was the same as he had heard from the cloud, but asked, "Why do you ask my name?" The man said, "I heard a voice from a cloud – whose water is here – to water so and so's garden, taking your name." He then asked him, "What is special that you do (to deserve such heavenly blessing)." The gardener said, "Since you have asked it, I divide whatever produce this garden gives me in three parts: I give one part in charity, spend one part for myself and my family, and reinvest one part in this garden." '

(*Muslim*: Abu Hurayrah)

18
No Charity is Too Small!

The Messenger of God, bpuh, said: 'Do not belittle even the smallest act of kindness, even if it were no more than meeting your brother with a smiling and cheerful face.'

(*Muslim*: Abu Dharr)

The Messenger of God, bpuh, said: 'O Muslim women, let no neighbour consider anything too insignificant to give to her neighbour, even if it be a sheep's trotter.'

(*Bukhari, Muslim*: Abu Hurayrah)

The Messenger of God, bpuh, said: 'If someone gives as charity as little as a single date from honest earnings – and God accepts only honest earnings – God takes it in His Right Hand, then makes it grow for the benefit of the charity-giver, just as one of you raises his foal, until it becomes as big as a mountain.'

(*Bukhari, Muslim*: Abu Hurayrah)

19
Generous Spending

The Messenger of God, bpuh, said: 'If I had a mountain of gold, I would not like to save any of it for more than three days, except something I put aside to pay debts.'

(*Bukhari*: Abu Hurayrah)

The Messenger of God, bpuh, said: 'Go on giving and do not count, for then God too will count whatever He gives you; and do not hoard wealth, for then God will withhold wealth from you; even give such small amounts as you can.'

(*Bukhari, Muslim*: Asma)

The Messenger of God, bpuh, said: 'A generous person is close to God, close to Paradise, close to people, and far from Hell. However a miserly person is far from God, far from Paradise, far from people, but close to Hell. God loves more an ignorant man who is generous than a worshipper who is miserly.'

(*Tirmidhi*: Abu Hurayrah)

20
You Never Lose

The Messenger of God, bpuh, said: 'If one gives charity, it does not diminish his wealth; if one forgives others, God bestows more honour on him; and if one humbles himself for God's Sake, He exalts him higher.'

(*Muslim*: Abu Hurayrah)

The Messenger of God, bpuh, said: 'A man said to himself, "I will give some charity today." He went out during the night and put his alms in the hand of a person, but he was a thief. The next morning, the word spread that last night alms had been given to a thief. The man said, "O God, all praise belongs to You – to a thief! I will again give some charity."

'Next night, he again went out, and this time put his alms in the hand of a woman, but she was a prostitute. The next morning, the word again spread that last night alms had been given to a prostitute. The man said, "O God, all praise belongs to You – to a prostitute! I will again give some charity."

'He again went out the next night, but this time he put his alms in the hand of a person who was rich. The next morning, people were again saying that last night alms had been given to a rich person. So the charitable man said, "O God, all praise belongs to You – to a thief, to a prostitute, to a rich man!"

'He then had a vision, and someone said to him: "As for your charity to a thief, it might get him to refrain from stealing. As for the prostitute, it might get her to refrain from prostitution. As for the rich man, he might take a lesson from it and spend of what God has given him." '

(*Bukhari, Muslim*: Abu Hurayrah)

4
Caring and Kindness

21
Golden Rules for Human Relations

The Prophet, bpuh, said: 'No one among you attains true faith, until he likes for his brother what he likes for himself.'

(*Bukhari, Muslim*: Anas)

The Messenger of God, bpuh, said: 'The believers in their mutual love, compassion and sympathy are like one body: when one of its parts suffers from some illness, the rest of the body shares its suffering with sleeplessness and fever.'

(*Bukhari, Muslim*: Nu'man ibn Bashir)

The Messenger of God, bpuh, said: 'Whoever relieves a believer from a distress, God will relieve him from one of his distresses on the Day of Resurrection. Whoever alleviates the hardship of a person in difficulty, God will alleviate his hardship in this world and the next. Whoever covers [the shortcomings, faults and sins of] a Muslim, God will cover him up in this world and the next. And remember, God will help a servant so long as the servant helps his brother.'

(*Muslim*: Abu Hurayrah)

The Messenger of God, bpuh, said: 'A Muslim is a brother to a Muslim. He neither wrongs him nor abandons him. Whoever cares for any need of his brother, God will care for his needs.'

(*Bukhari, Muslim*: Ibn Umar)

The Messenger of God, bpuh, said: 'Whoever fulfils the need of someone from my people in order to please him, he pleases me, and he who pleases me pleases God, and he who pleases God will be admitted by Him into Paradise.'

(*Baihaqi*: Anas)

The Messenger of God, bpuh, said: 'I saw a man strolling in Paradise. He was given this reward for cutting down a tree which had blocked a road and caused inconvenience to people.'

(*Muslim*: Abu Hurayrah)

22
Caring for Animals

The Messenger of God, bpuh, said: 'A woman was punished and thrown into Hell-fire on account of her cat. She kept it tied up till it died of hunger: neither she gave it something to eat or drink, nor let it go so that it could eat things on earth.'

(*Bukhari, Muslim*: Ibn Umar)

The Messenger of God, bpuh, has forbidden to make an animal a target for arrow shooting.

(Bukhari, Muslim: Anas)

The Messenger of God, bpuh, forbade the beating or tattooing of an animal on its face.

(Muslim)

Once the Messenger of God, bpuh, passed by a camel who was so emaciated that his belly seemed to have disappeared. He said, 'Fear God regarding the animals who cannot speak. Ride on them while they are healthy, and eat of them when they are healthy.'

(Abu Dawud: Sahl ibn 'Amr)

23
Caring for Servants

The Messenger of God, bpuh, said: 'Slaves [and servants] are your brothers, whom God has placed under you. So whoever has some brother of his under him he should feed him what he eats himself, and clothe him with what he himself wears; and (remember) do not give him a task that is too much for him, but if you have to give, then you must help him.'

(*Bukhari, Muslim*: Abu Dharr)

The Messenger of God, bpuh, said: 'When your servant brings you your meal, but you do not invite him to sit with you to eat, then at least give him some food for himself, for it is he who suffered the heat of the fire and took pains to prepare the food.'

(*Muslim*: Abu Hurayrah)

A man asked the Prophet, bpuh: 'How often should we forgive our servants?' The Prophet, bpuh, kept silent. He repeated his question again, and again. The third time, the Prophet, bpuh, said: 'Forgive him seventy [that is, many, many] times every day.'

(*Abu Dawud*: Abdullah ibn Umar)

The Messenger of God, bpuh, said: 'Whoever has a female slave, and he educates her, treats her well, then frees her and marries her, he has a double reward.'

(*Bukhari*: Abu Burdah)

24
Caring for the Family

The Messenger of God, bpuh, said: 'Anyone who desires his earnings to grow and his life to be prolonged should treat his relatives well.'

(*Bukhari, Muslim*: Anas)

The Messenger of God, bpuh, said: 'One who breaks the ties of relations with his relatives shall not enter Paradise.'

(*Bukhari, Muslim*: Jubayr)

The Messenger of God, bpuh, said: 'A person who merely reciprocates when doing good, is not really the one who maintains ties with his relatives, but the one who does good and maintains relations even if others do not do good, is a good relative.'

(*Bukhari*: Abdullah ibn 'Amr)

25
Caring for Parents and Children

The Messenger of God, bpuh, said: 'No father can give a better gift to his children than providing them with a good education.'

(*Baihaqi*: Ayub ibn Musa)

26
Caring for Women

The Messenger of God, bpuh, said: 'The most perfect in faith among the believers are those who possess the best morals, and the best among you are those who are kindest to their wives.'

(*Tirmidhi*: Abu Hurayrah)

The Messenger of God, bpuh, said: 'The best of you is he who is best to his family, and I am the best among you towards my family.'

(*Tirmidhi*: A'ishah)

Giving a sermon during the Farewell Pilgrimage, the Messenger of God, bpuh, said: 'Fear God in matters relating to women. And act kindly towards them.'

(*Bukhari, Muslim*: Jabir, Abu Hurayrah)

The Messenger of God, bpuh, said: 'If one has a daughter and he does not bury her alive, nor slights her or prefers his other children (that is, the male ones) to her, God will admit him into Paradise.'

(*Abu Dawud*: Ibn 'Abbas)

The Messenger of God, bpuh, said: 'Anyone who looks after and brings up three daughters, or sisters, educates them well, treats them with compassion, until God makes them self-sufficient, God guarantees him Paradise.' A man asked, 'Suppose there are only two?' He said, 'Yes, two as well.' People said, 'And if there be only one?' He said, 'Yes, even if there is only one.'

(*Sharh al-Sunnah*: Ibn 'Abbas)

27
Caring for Non-Muslims

The mother of Asma, the daughter of Abu Bakr, was still a polytheist when she came to visit Asma during the time of the Muslims' peace treaty with the Quraysh. Asma asked the Prophet, bpuh, 'O Messenger of God, my mother has come to see me. Should I receive her and treat her with all the affection that is her due?' He said, 'Yes, treat her with full affection.'

(Bukhari, Muslim: Asma)

The Messenger of God, bpuh, said: 'One who kills a non-Muslim whose protection is pledged, will never smell the fragrance of Jannah, even though it reaches as far as forty years distance.'

(Bukhari: Ibn Umar)

28
Caring for the Neighbour

The Messenger of God, bpuh, said: 'By God, he cannot be a true believer! By God, he cannot be a true believer! By God, he cannot be a true believer!' When asked who it is, he said, 'The one from whose harmful conduct his neighbour is not safe.'

(Bukhari, Muslim: Abu Hurayrah)

The Messenger of God, bpuh, said: 'Angel Gabriel kept on pressing upon me the rights of a neighbour so much so that I thought he would make him an heir.'

(Bukhari, Muslim: A'ishah)

The Messenger of God, bpuh, said: 'He is not a true believer who eats his fill while his neighbour is hungry.'

(Baihaqi: Ibn 'Abbas)

A man said, 'O Messenger of God, bpuh, such and such woman has a reputation for engaging very much in Prayers, Fasting and Almsgiving, but she hurts her neighbours with her tongue quite often.' He said, 'She will go to Hell.' Then he said, 'O Messenger of God, bpuh, such and such woman engages in only a little Prayer, Fasting and Almsgiving and gives just a few pieces of cheese in charity, but she does not hurt her neighbours with her tongue.' He said, 'She will go to Paradise.'

(*Ahmad, Baihaqi*: Abu Hurayrah)

The Messenger of God, bpuh, said: 'When three of you are together, let two of you not talk between themselves ignoring the third – until you are among a larger number of people – so as not to hurt him.'

(*Bukhari, Muslim*: Abdullah ibn Mas'ud)

29
Caring for the Sick

The Messenger of God, bpuh, said: 'When a Muslim visits a sick brother, he continues to pick the fruits of Paradise till he returns.'

(*Muslim*: Thauban)

When one of us fell sick, the Messenger of God, bpuh, used to put his right hand on our forehead, and say, 'Remove the hardship, Lord of mankind, and give healing. You are the Healer. There is no healing but from You, a healing which leaves no illness behind.'

(*Bukhari, Muslim*: A'ishah)

The Messenger of God, bpuh, said: 'Whatever hardship, pain, anxiety, grief, injury, or sorrow, afflicts a Muslim – even if it be as little as the prick of a thorn – God makes it an atonement for his sins.'

(*Bukhari, Muslim*: Abu Sa'id al-Khudri)

The Messenger of God, bpuh, said: 'If a servant of God is used to doing good in serving Him, and then becomes ill, the angel with him is told, "Record for him all the good deeds which he used to do when he was well, until I cure him or he dies." '

(*Sharh al-Sunnah*: Ibn 'Amr)

30
General Behaviour

The Messenger of God, bpuh, said: 'Let him who believes in God and the Last Day either speak good or keep silent; let him who believes in God and the Last Day honour his neighbour; and let him who believes in God and the Last Day honour his guest.'

(*Bukhari, Muslim*: Abu Hurayrah)

The Messenger of God, bpuh, said: 'Sometimes when I begin the Prayer I intend to make it long;

but, then, I hear some child cry, and I shorten my Prayer, thinking of the mother's great distress because of her child's crying.'

(*Bukhari*: Abu Qatada)

The Messenger of God, bpuh, said: 'He does not belong to us Muslims who is not kind to our young and does not respect our old.'

(*Tirmidhi*: Ibn 'Abbas)

The Messenger of God, bpuh, said: 'He who cares for the widowed and the needy is like the one who struggles and fights in the way of God, or like the one who prays all night and fasts all day.'

(*Bukhari, Muslim*: Abu Hurayrah)

The Messenger of God, bpuh, said: 'It is an excellence of a person's faith that he is not concerned with anything that does not matter for him.'

(*Tirmidhi*: Abu Hurayrah)

31
Helping the Oppressor

The Messenger of God, bpuh, said: 'Help your brother, whether he is doing wrong to others, or is being wronged.'

A man protested: 'O Messenger of God, bpuh, I can understand helping one who is being wronged, but how can I help him when he is doing wrong?'

The Prophet, bpuh, replied: 'Stop him from doing wrong: this is your help to him.'

(*Bukhari, Muslim*: Anas)

5
Morals and Piety

32
Trust and Promise

Seldom did the Messenger of God, bpuh, address us without saying: 'He who is not trustworthy has no faith; he who does not keep his word has no religion.'
(*Baihaqi*: Anas)

33
Backbiting

The Messenger of God, bpuh, said: 'Backbiting means saying something that will offend your brother.'

Someone asked: 'But what, if what I say about him is true?'

He replied: 'If that which you say about him is true, you have backbited him; but if it is not true, then you have slandered him as well.'

(*Muslim*: Abu Hurayrah)

34
Pride

The Messenger of God, bpuh, said: 'No one will be admitted into Paradise who has even a tiny grain of pride in his heart.'

A man asked him: 'But what if someone likes to dress well and put on good sandals?'

He replied: 'Truly God is beautiful, and He loves beauty. Pride is to disdain the truth, and to belittle and despise other people.'

(*Muslim*: Abdullah ibn Mas'ud)

35
Self Help

The Messenger of God, bpuh, said: 'It is better for one if he takes his rope, gets up early in the morning to go into the mountains, cuts and brings a load of firewood on his back, and sells it, and eats from this and gives charity from it so that God preserves his self-respect. This is better than that he should beg of people who may sometime give him something, but may also sometime refuse to.'

(*Bukhari*: Zubayr)

The Messenger of God, bpuh, said: 'No one eats better food than what he earns by the labour of his own hands. Indeed God's Prophet David, bpuh, used to eat from the labour of his own hand.'

He also said: 'David, in fact, never ate but from the work of his own hands.'

(*Bukhari*: Miqdam)

36
The Problem of Evil

The Messenger of God, bpuh, said: 'How wonderful is the case of a believer! There is good for him in whatever happens to him – and none apart from him enjoys this blessing. If he receives some bounty, he is grateful to God, and this bounty brings good to him. And if some adversity befalls him, he is patient, and this affliction, too, brings good to him.'

(*Muslim*: Suhayb)

37
Seeking Knowledge

The Messenger of God, bpuh, said: 'If one travels in search of knowledge, God will make him travel to Paradise; the angels, being highly pleased with him, spread their wings over the seeker of knowledge; everything in the heavens and on earth, even the fish in the depths of water, seek forgiveness for a scholar; and the superiority of a learned man over one engaged in ritual worship is like that of a full moon over the rest of the stars.'

(*Ahmad*: Abu Darda)

38
Responsibility

The Messenger of God, bpuh, said: 'Everyone of you is a shepherd, everyone of you is responsible for his flock. A ruler is shepherd over his people; he is accountable for their welfare. A man is shepherd over his family, he is accountable for their welfare. A woman is shepherdess over her husband's household and children, she is accountable for their welfare. A man's servant is shepherd over his master's property, he is accountable for it. Be careful! All of you are shepherds, and all of you shall be accountable for their flocks.'

(*Bukhari, Muslim*: Abdullah ibn Umar)

39
Accountability

The Prophet, bpuh, said: 'On the Day of Judgement no child of Adam will move from the presence of God, unless he has answered about five things: *(firstly)* in what pursuits and work did he spend his time; *(secondly)* for what ends did he use up his mental and physical energies; *(thirdly)* by what means did he earn his wealth; *(fourthly)* and, how did he spend it; and *(fifthly)* how far did he act according to what he knew was right.'

(Tirmidhi: Ibn Mas'ud)

The Messenger of God, bpuh, said: 'Each one of you will most surely stand before God, with no veil between you and God, and no interpreter to interpret for you. Then God shall say, "Did I not give you wealth?" And you will say, "Yes." Then God shall say, "Did I not send a Messenger to you?" And you will say, "Yes."

'Then you will look to your right but see nothing

but Fire [of your deeds]; and you will look to your left but see nothing but Fire [of your deeds].

'So each of you should ward off the Fire from yourself, even if it be by giving half a date in charity. And if you cannot find even that, then by a good word.'

(*Bukhari:* 'Adi ibn Hatim)

The Messenger of God, bpuh, said: 'Whoever is guilty of doing some wrong against a fellow human being, whether in regard to his honour or anything else, he should obtain his forgiveness before the Day of Judgement, when there will be no money to pay for it. If he has any good deeds to his credit, they will be taken away from him to the extent of his wrong-doing. And if he has no good deeds, the sins of the wronged-one will be taken and put on him.'

(*Bukhari*: Abu Hurayrah)

40
Merciful Judgement

The Messenger of God, bpuh, said: 'No one will be saved (from the Hell-fire and admitted into the Paradise) by his deeds alone.' When asked, 'Not even you! O Messenger of God, bpuh', he said, 'Yes, not even me. Unless God covers me with His mercy. So, try your best to keep to the right path, adopt moderation, make your life-journey easy by travelling in the morning, in the evening, and during part of the night, and always remember moderation, always abide by moderation. Thus you will reach your destination.'

(*Bukhari, Muslim*: Abu Hurayrah)

The Messenger of God, bpuh, said: 'God has a hundred mercies. Only one part of them has He sent down among the jinn, humankind, animals and insects. It is because of this that they are kind to one another, show mercy to one another, it is because of it that a wild animal is kind to its young.

But God has kept ninety-nine mercies with Him, by which He will show mercy to His servants on the Day of Resurrection.'

(*Bukhari, Muslim*: Abu Hurayrah)

The Messenger of God, bpuh, said: 'God will call a believer near Him and cover him, and say, "Are you aware of this sin! Are you aware of that sin!" He will admit every sin, "Yes, my Lord." This will continue until He makes him admit all his sins, and he thinks that he is going to perish. God will then say, "I kept them hidden for you in the world, and I forgive them today." '

(*Bukhari, Muslim*: Ibn Umar)

The Messenger of God, bpuh, said: 'A man never did any good deed in his life. When death came, he asked his sons to burn his body and scatter half of his ashes on the land, and half in the sea – swearing by God that were God to have power over him, He would punish him as He would punish no one in this world. When he died, his sons did what he had asked. But God ordered the sea and it gathered what ashes were in it, and ordered the land and it too gathered what was in it. He then asked him, "Why did you do this?" He replied, "Out of Your fear, O Lord! You know very well." Upon this, He forgave him.'

(*Bukhari, Muslim*: Abu Hurayrah)